Catspirations

SWEET & SIMPLE TRUTHS FROM OUR FELINE FRIENDS

Catspirations

SWEET & SIMPLE TRUTHS FROM OUR FELINE FRIENDS

■ WILLOW CREEK PRESS®

Published by Willow Creek Press, Inc.
P.O. Box 147, Minocqua, Wisconsin 54548

Printed in China

THE BEST
View
COMES AFTER THE HARDEST
Climb

IT DOESN'T MATTER HOW

Slowly

YOU GO AS LONG AS YOU DON'T STOP

THROW

Kindness

AROUND LIKE

Confetti

Embrace
THE
Journey

YOU CAN'T CROSS

The Sea

BY MERELY STANDING AND

Staring

AT THE WATER

Bloom

WHERE YOU ARE

Planted

Sometimes

YOU NEED TO LOOK AT LIFE FROM A DIFFERENT

Perspective

Taste YOUR Words

BEFORE YOU SPIT THEM OUT

TRY TO BE A

Rainbow

IN SOMEONE'S

Cloud

LIFE IS

Short

EAT DESSERT

First

Do Less WITH MORE Focus

STORMS MAKE
Flowers
TAKE DEEPER ROOT

IMAGINATION

Will Take

YOU EVERYWHERE

GREET THE People YOU LOVE WITH A Smile

DREAM

Bigger

THAN YOU CAN

Doubt

IN A WORLD OF PLAIN
Bagels
BE A SPRINKLED
Doughnut

LET YOUR

Dreams

OUTGROW THE SHOES OF YOUR

Expectations

Failure is success in progress

Obstacles

Do Not Block The

Path

They Are The Path

ALONE WE CAN DO SO LITTLE

Together

WE CAN DO SO MUCH

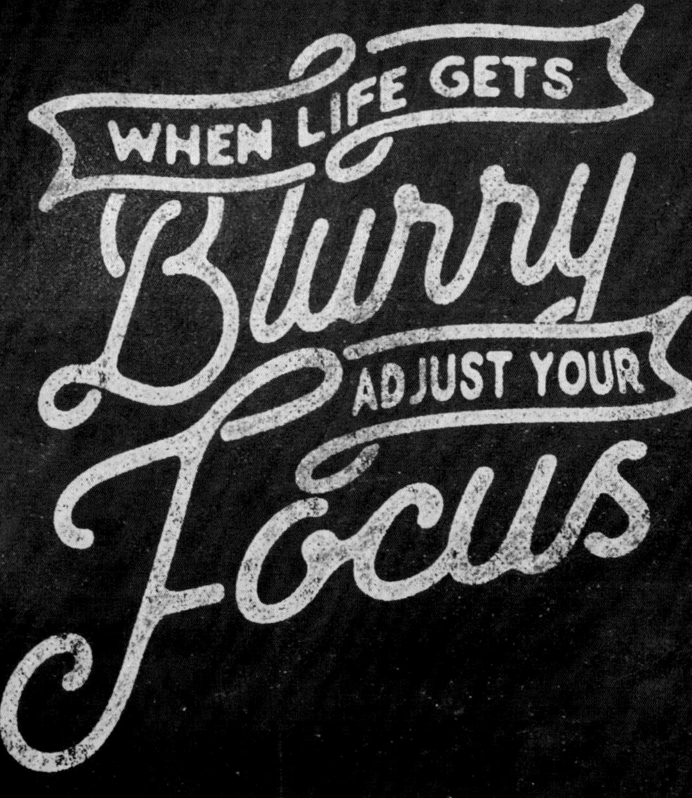
WHEN LIFE GETS
Blurry
ADJUST YOUR
Focus

ONCE YOU CHOOSE

Hope

ANYTHING IS POSSIBLE

CREATIVE
Minds
ARE NEVER
Tidy

Sometimes THE ONLY WAY OUT IS Through

THERE ARE ALWAYS

Flowers

FOR THOSE WHO WANT TO SEE THEM

IT TAKES

Strength

TO BE GENTLE AND KIND

ONE DAY OR

Day One

YOU DECIDE

YOU ARE MORE

Capable

THAN YOU KNOW

Kindness COSTS Nothing

THE
Struggle
IS ONLY PART OF THE
Story

KEEP YOUR FACE TO THE

Sunshine

AND YOU CANNOT SEE THE SHADOWS

BE

Proud

OF YOUR ACCOMPLISHMENTS

WHEN YOU WANT TO

Give Up

REMEMBER WHY YOU STARTED

Limits are for Those who need them

EVEN BAD Chapters CAN MAKE A STORY END WELL

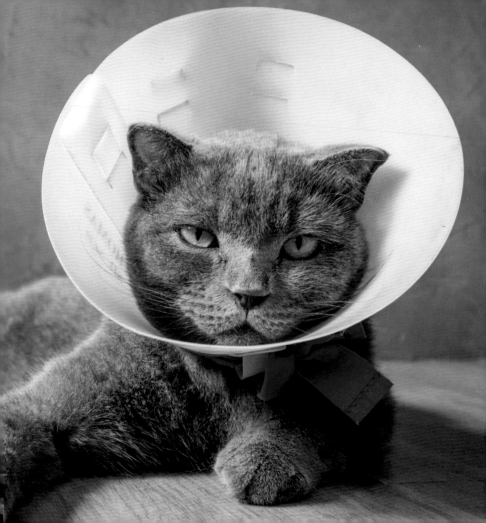

Difficult ROADS LEAD TO Beautiful DESTINATIONS

IT TAKES A

Long Time

TO GROW AN OLD FRIEND

FEAR IS Temporary REGRET IS Forever